FINDING YOUR
NITCH

FINDING YOUR
NITCH

A Guide for Stay at Home Fathers

Kelvin Alexander

Copyright © 2020 by Kelvin Alexander.

Library of Congress Control Number:		2020914620
ISBN:	Hardcover	978-1-6641-2312-0
	Softcover	978-1-6641-2311-3
	eBook	978-1-6641-2310-6

All rights reserved. No part of this book may be reproduced or transmitted in any form or by any means, electronic or mechanical, including photocopying, recording, or by any information storage and retrieval system, without permission in writing from the copyright owner.

Any people depicted in stock imagery provided by Getty Images are models, and such images are being used for illustrative purposes only.
Certain stock imagery © Getty Images.

Print information available on the last page.

Rev. date: 08/11/2020

To order additional copies of this book, contact:
Xlibris
844-714-8691
www.Xlibris.com
Orders@Xlibris.com
817953

TABLE OF CONTENTS

Acknowledgements and Dedications vii
Introduction ix

1   The Folks 1

    The Kids 3
    The Wives (Feelings) 5
    17 – 25 7
    Homosexuality 11

2   The Fellas 13

    The Fellas 15
    Spin 17
    Junior 21
    Kane 25
    Rome 27

3   The Foundation 31

    Certainty 33
    The Nitch 37
    In Conclusion 39

Acknowledgements and Dedications

I'd like to dedicate this book to the many, many people who have guided, understood and withstood my idiosyncrasies over the years. Of course I couldn't mention them all but there are a precious few who deserve mentioning.

My mother, Ms. Eula Mae Alexander, might I say, the great Eula Alexander who raised 10 children on her own and today each of them are hardworking, productive American Citizens. My tribute to mama is based on her steadfast insistence that we succeed. She never accepted an excuse, never wavered in her Christian beliefs and always and I mean always prayed fervently for each of us. Whenever I expressed to mama that I was "bored', she'd snap back, "then go read a book". I can't tell you how many times I listened to that simple, straightforward suggestion. This ultimately led me to become the person I have today. God bless my Mama!!!!.

Mrs. Denise Alexander, my wife and the mother of my children, more than anybody else, this remarkable woman is responsible for what is in this book. Mrs. Alexander (Sweetie) which I like to call her, is the most discipline, understanding and moralistic person of anyone I have ever met. I thank god everyday that he sent her to me at the most tumultuous time in my life. I was a young undisciplined college student, who needed emotional direction and focus. During our nearly three decades of marriage, sweetie has been my guiding light. She has helped me manage the various passages of my life and has always kept me on an even keel even when I strayed from my focus. She never allowed me to get too high or too low and has been the real head of our wonderful household. I could honestly say without any equivocation that I "would not be alive today" if not for the advice, companionship, love and understanding of this great lady. Sweetie, I owe my life to you and words cannot explain my love, dedication and commitment to you. If god gave me another hundred years in this body, I will spend each one of them right by your side.

My children, who have given me unconditional love and affection from day one. I wish that one day I can return even half of that love that you had so unselfishly given me. I am so proud and happy with the progress you all have made in your lives and I am writing this book for you. You see, I want fathers from future generations to look back and learn what I have learned from you. How children can help their fathers and how my children's children can have a blueprint for fatherhood only because of what my children did for me. I love and am forever indebted to you for your part in designing my life.

Introduction

There are scores of books that detail the perils, pitfalls and joys of fatherhood. Some make the case better than others and some are based on pure fantasy. So why in the world would anyone want to write another one? Well because the statements about these books making the case are simply not true. I have found that if books on fatherhood did not depict fathers as drunkards, fathers who beat their wives or abuse their children, fathers who molest and torment young people while hiding under a too good to be true façade or fathers that display sociopath behavior behind closed doors. There would not be any books about fathers at all. Some books have even portrayed father's as religious zealots with a diabolical personality underneath.

The Nitch will be a different book on fatherhood, mainly because it will be presented as a workbook on fatherhood. It will be presented by fathers for men and yes women who are fathers today tomorrow and or yesterday. This book will document tried and true techniques made by men who have made a conscious effort to guide their families through some very tough times and identify some critical turning points in fatherhood which I believe all fathers at some point will confront.

The Nitch will display chronicles of the lives and experiences of fathers whose only hope is the maintenance of their families and the mental, physical and spiritual fortification of their children.

You won't find any complicated scientific methodologies on parenting in this book. Even though there is some science it is science which brings understanding to a particular issue or situation. What you will find is specific points from fathers who have decided that beyond any costs they will sacrifice, work and continue to create a complete unbroken family unit. Please learn and enjoy.

Section I

The Folks

The Kids

Do not ever leave your children for any reason at all!!!!!!. Unless you and your wife are biting, scratching, kicking, slapping or punching at each other, wild horses should not be able to drive you away from your children. So you ask, why stay together just for the children? My answer, why not? When you have children you have a responsibility for their well being. You are responsible for their food, clothing and shelter. Of course that isn't enough to stop you from leaving. So listen to this scientific reasoning. Your children are your DNA and would you leave your DNA just lying anywhere? Let me give you a scenario to explain just what I am talking about. Suppose you had the ability to remove your arms every night and leave them on the shelf before you went to sleep. You would do this every day so that you can sleep better. What would happen if one day you went to work and left you arms on the dresser, you actually forgot to reattach your arms that day because you woke up late, hurried out of the house and forgot your arms. How effective would you be at work that day? You would probably have to go back home get your arms so that you could do a good day's work or just sit around all day at your job doing nothing. That's exactly what happens when you leave your DNA just lying around anywhere. You become useless because some your vital parts are missing.

Imagine functioning during this accelerated time period, (you know that we live in an accelerated time period), with your children going to school everyday, growing and forming before your very eyes. Imagine being in a household where you never lose sight of the going ons in this world. Imagine being on top of everything that is swirling around throughout this city, state, country and world. I guarantee you that if you don't have your children in your everyday life, you will be so behind the times that a turtle could out run and you will eventually have the intellect of an after dinner mint. You think that your children need you, you might be right, but you need them just as much. Children supply the kinetic energy in your life that connects you to the universe. They bring back the necessary information that identifies all of the advances happening around you. Children learn the new lingo, they learn the new mathematics, they learn the new technologies and they bring that entire stuff home to you. Children keep you new, up-to-date and improve your possibilities for success. As a man you naturally thrive on new challenges, children will bring you new challenges everyday! With those new challenges will come the ability to meet them? You need children to live, to grow and most importantly to come to grips with your humanity.

Lesson One- Children are your DNA, don't ever leave your DNA lying around just anywhere.

Lesson Two- Children help you to live and become a more successful man.

THE WIVES (FEELINGS)

Once I had a very special conversation with my wife. At the time we had been married a little more than 5 years and I thought that it was time to come to grips with some very important emotions. You see, as a person who was never very able to love completely, mainly because of my sexual adventurism. I realized that I at this time in my life that I had fallen completely in love with this woman, so I had to have a conversation with her and remind her of her responsibilities in this whole "feelings thing". I have some very practical methods that should be used when falling in love with a woman. I realized that this woman has the power of my heart in her hands. She can protect my heart or destroy it. So I wanted to very carefully explain this to her and I wanted to let other men know how this works.

Firstly, I explained that my ability to take on the burden of true love was limited. That I was often afraid of love, because when you love, you place the care of your heart in another persons hands. Ladies let me be clear, when a man falls in love. I mean really in love, they fall hard. That means that the person we fall in love with has our emotional stability in their hands. That's right ladies, you can make him or break him. This means that any time you display any displeasure about anything, I mean anything (if he truly loves you) it hits him like a ton of bricks. For example, you might come home one night and your wife might start complaining about the way you left you socks or the bathroom floor or anything extremely simple. If that happens ladies please take a minute and sooth you husband back to commonality. Why because he is injured emotionally and he needs to be brought back. You have to take a minute and take the stake out of his heart that you just put in there just because you complained a little bit. When ever you criticize this man he feels like he has lost his grip on the world. A man who truly loves you, never, ever, ever wants to disappoint you in any way. So wives, be careful how you approach criticism.

Lesson #1: A man, who falls in love, really falls in love hard

Lesson #2 Wives, be careful how you approach criticism.

17 – 25

    Often times I have had the opportunity to observe male behavior at certain crossroads in their lives. These crossroads from this day forward shall be referred to as "Vacuums" Now the scientific definition of vacuum is the absence of air and because there is an absence of air vacuums usually suck things into them to feel a void. For the benefit of this discussion I have identified three major vacuums in the lives of male children, ages 1-5, ages 10-13 and ages 17-25.

    Now as a child under the age of five, all manner of things which beret you are things which creates and builds your personality. These years are called the formative years, which basically mean these are the years "that you are formed". Your tastes, your likes your dislikes, your ability to identify your family, friends and the coming of school learning are things that materialize during this vacuum. In fact there are those who believe that any misstep during this vacuum will affect you for the rest of your life. That may be true and I am sure that there are many studies which can show proof of that statement, but I believe that this vacuum to be the least important as it relates to male children. I believe that almost anything that occurs during this vacuum can be overcome later in your life.

    Talking about the 10-13 vacuum is quite interesting. Most males discover their sexuality during this time, they begin to realize the role that sports and sportsmanship plays in their lives, and most importantly men usually decide what course their lives will take during this vacuum. This vacuum sucks in girls and friends and all of the other fascinating things which pop culture have to offer. If I could choose the happiest time of my pre-adult life, I would definitely choose the 10-13 vacuum, man that time was fun. I started paying attention to girls and all that which excites them. Even though I learned little about girls at that time I was just happy to discover that god had added sweet voluptuous females as a part of my life. It was a time when the only thing that was mandatory in my life was school. I could play ball all the time and not have to worry about paying bills. Mama fed me, clothed me and provided me with shelter. I believe I grew more intellectually, spiritually and physically during this time that at any other time in my life. There are some real hazards which can occur during his vacuum. If you are not careful you can easily become a victim of drugs, crime and sexual deviancy. Why? Because you are too young and stupid to realize the difference between right and wrong. Its not that you don't know the difference between right and wrong, during this time you just don't seem to differentiate properly. You just want to have fun. Myself, I was just lucky enough to have a praying mother, who reminded me of things every time I walked out the front door. Those little reminders used to reverberate throughout my mind all day long, thank you mama. So don't be afraid to constantly remind your children of the perils that they might encounter.

Now with the vacuum 17 – 25, I see a totally different story. Because you start out as a high school graduate, you want money in your pocket, you're probably as big as you'll ever become and you are confused by everything.

The 17-25 vacuum is the most difficult time of your life. Well, I think I am a man but every time I say so, some grown person reminds me that I'm still a child. I try to be a child but some starry eyed teenager calls me an old man. Most programs are either for the very young or the very old. Nobody really believes that I am grown but most people start treating me like I am supposed to be taking care of myself. So I attempt to do that by any means necessary, sometimes at my own detriment. This vacuum seems to draw all of the negative things into my life, and since I am at a certain age most of my advice comes from my peers, who are going through the same things. So I can't seem to sort it all out. How do you sort it out? Simply fill the vacuum with certain things. It might sound too easy, but it is not easy, but it is quite simple. Fill this vacuum with school, church, and or volunteerism. This is sooooo important I have to say that again, SCHOOL, CHURCH AND VOLUNTEERISM.

If you really thought about it, those types of activities are the ones which are always welcoming to anyone. If you don't want to go to college, go to a trade school and learn something like pluming, carpentry, heating and air conditioning auto mechanic training, etc. These under utilized fields of study are in tremendous demand today and offer some exciting opportunities for successful earnings. I can't tell you how I feel every time I have to call the plumber. I know that just for him to walk in the front door it will cost me $100.00.

I am not one to advocate for any particular religion, I just feel that at this point in your life, that if you get in touch with your spiritual side you can be prepared to handle the problems that this specific vacuum draws into your life. Spirituality puts you in touch with forces which you can believe are greater that you. Life is an endless cycle of failure and successes, mostly failures. When you fail yourself which you surely will, when you family fails you, which they surely will, and when your friends fails you which is an absolute definite, you can look upon something which you are taught will never fail you; the spiritual being that now encompasses you faith. This spiritual connection is incapable of failure and it will be there when you need it most, particularly during the 17 -25 vacuum. Believe me brothers it works, I testify to this from personal experience.

Finally, there are thousands of organizations that would love to have a young, strong, intelligent and open minded persons like you come and volunteer to help them with their causes, nuff said, do it.

Homosexuality

When contemplating this very controversial topic, I was struck by the number of people who had hard and fast opinions about it but never really took the time for any types of intellectual discussions on the subject. I myself have examined any number of major changes on the American landscape and found some very interesting conclusions as it relate to the male perspective. Because whether it was the Civil Rights Movement, the Women's Movement and today the Universal Health Care Movement or any major social movement in American History. It seemed as though it was the human male that was nearly always at the forefront of the opposition. In other words the men in our society seemed to be the ones who are most resistant to change. I am not sure what that means. It could mean that women are more tolerant, or because men are "at the top of the food chain" any changes in the life style in the country might affect the way that the "top dogs" live, or it could mean any number of things. Since this book was written mainly as a manual to help men understand and solve some of the situations that might affect their relationships, I felt this subject area is certainly one of the changes in society that men had to reconcile with. Why, because as a father, grandfather, uncle, and son, I might have to confront the reality of Homosexuality within my household or extended family. With this discussion I am attempting to offer a measure of clarity to men. Not to justify Homosexuality nor to condemn it. God knows there have been enough opinions on both sides of that issue. But to begin creating the facility where fathers can continue to love and nurture their children. As you read on I wish to remind you that I am not a social scientist or a scientist of any kind, I am just relating my observations and suggestions on this topic

In Natural Selection there is a term called Predation. Predation is the theory where species are controlled through a predator/prey relationship. Predation is used to include interactions in which an organism consumes all or part of another. This includes predator-prey, herbivore-plant, and parasite-host interactions. These linkages are the primary movers of energy through the food chains. They are an important factor in the ecology of populations, determining the mortality rate of both the predator and the prey.

On the planet Earth, nature (God) has placed any number of controls in place. It has been said that the great epidemic in Medieval Europe was caused because human beings hunted down and killed all of the natural predators of rodents and other vermin, thereby leading to the spread of gems and disease. These killings of predators and the spreading of gems and disease led to the death of tens of millions of people. The tiny aphid, an insect that multiplies at an alarming rate, can actually cover the entire Earth in a matter of months if not for the lady bug and other insects which eat thousands of them everyday. Great White Sharks are said to be vital to containing the Seal populations of the South Pole. Insects can overrun our entire planet if not for the diligent work of bats which eat them constantly. Bats are so important, that in some parts of this country, to kill one is a crime. It is also true that many farmers cultivate bats to protect their fields from swarming insects. It is also believed by some that the destruction of frogs and their habitats have led to the proliferation of insect borne diseases like West Nile Virus. Mother Nature (God) has placed just the right amount of predator/prey combinations on this planet to control the over populations of all species. The only species on this planet that doesn't seem to have a natural predator is Human Beings.

In human populations disease has for many centuries controlled the over population of the world. But with the advent of better and improved medical techniques and medicines, the human population has continued to grow. There have been many unnatural population control mechanisms incorporated into population control, such as wars which have led to the deaths of millions over the years. But as it relates to Natural Selection the human population has continued to expand and explode. Hence my hypothesis.

The only thing that homosexuals cannot do naturally is procreate. Gender-specific relationships are not meant to re-produce or perpetuate the species. In fact, I predict that someday Homosexuality will help stabilize human populations to a manageable level. So, I believe that Homosexuality is a phenomenon of Natural Selection. This natural process is ever growing and serves a natures way of stabilizing the growth of the only uncontrolled species on the planet, human beings.

Remember, I don't give this explanation as a justification of Homosexuality, nor is it meant as a reason to condone the practice. As a Heterosexual Male with children, I have come to the realization that I might have to face that fact that one of my children or grand children is a Homosexual. I am not a scientist or making any type of scientific analysis. I am observing the real, and in observing the real, I wish to help men like me who are fathers, find a natural reason to keep loving and nurturing our children.

Section II

The Fellas

THE FELLAS

One of the things that I felt must go into the development of this book is the actual real life experiences of men who like myself had been married to the same woman for more than 20 years. Their prospective along with my prospective, I believe, will give the readers a greater understanding of the message that I am trying to convey. This is, that you can stay together, you can stay with your children, you can make a conscious effort to keep your family together and that you can be happy doing it.

The fellas are a compilation of stories which have been written in real life. It has been written with the exact words of the fellas and has hopefully added to the discussion of this book. It was probably the most interesting part of my investigation and analysis as I truly believe that being happy in long term relationships is a function of process and doesn't happen by accident. That's if you want your relationship to succeed you can make it happen. Just listen to the messages of the fellas.

Finally, this section was created by the asking of a few specific questions. What is your philosophy of marriage? What steps did you take to make sure that you marriage lasted through the trials and tribulations? Describe some of the major turning points in your marriage? How did the introduction of children into you relationship effect the relationship between you and your wife? And finally, what advice can you give to men who now are either deciding to enter into a long term relationship or are now struggling to keep their relationships together? The responses were often fascinating and sometimes surprising. As they described the loves of their lives and their never ending attempts to keep their relationships sacred and secure, I felt even more impressed with what can happen in relationships and how simple it really is, I never said it was easy, just simple), if you try.

I really appreciated their candor and their willingness to express themselves in such explicit terms. Introducing THE FELLAS, learn.

Spin

    This young man and his wife have been married for 25 plus years. He has decided to share his views on how we can help young people stay with their families through thick and thin. Listen very carefully.

    Marriage involves dealing with other personalities. You must know that she is feeling a certain way, not specifically what she is feeling, but know what **way** she is feeling, either up or down. You must know this so now you have a inkling on how you can adjust your emotions and actions accordingly. Women are very complicated so you never know what they are thinking just HOW they are thinking. Men are simple, we wear our feelings on our shoulders, so they are very easy to observe. Women can read us, they can read us very easily and they know if we are sincere. If you want to be successful in her eyes you must focus on the personality and learn to love it. You must be able to look into her face and know if she is feeling a certain way. If you make a mistake, you must be prepared for it to eventually show up, so prepare yourself, especially if it was something wrong. So when the arguing starts I would rather role up into the fetal position before I argue back. Someone must **always** decide not to argue.

    I believe the main reason I stayed married is that whenever there is a problem in my marriage, I focused on the one thing that made me fall in love with her from the beginning. I always go back to that one small special thing and it keeps me stationery. It usually is love at first site, so you can bear anything if you just go back to that one thing inside that caused you to marry her in the first place. You hold on to that very special thing and nothing. I believe nothing will ever come between you and your wife. That special thing will always be running through your very being and is the foundation of your relationship. Even if your wife cannot cook or stays in the store too long, which I hate, not even those things will come between you. If you hold on to that special thing, nothing will be able to stop your relationship. If you don't have that special thing you will break up over some simple things like cooking or sex. But if you have that special thing, the food will always be great and the sex will always be good.

Complaints are not that serious, so you should never take these things seriously. You see, we never have to do anything right, I learn from you, you learn from me, we get better together. Just hold on to that thing that made you fall in love in the first place. The average woman doesn't know what she wants specifically, just hold on until she discovers what she discovers what she wants. Because when she does the marriage will role along very smoothly. Infidelity in a marriage is overrated, it should not affect the way you love each other, all it is, is sex. She will forgive you for having an affair and you will learn how to forgive her. Women get emotional about sex and she needs to be forgiven. Remember, once you get that woman in your corner, I mean really get her in your corner, you can accomplish anything.

Black women have had a history of humiliation, disgrace and hurt, so that puts them in the defensive position. You will never understand her because of what she had to go through. So when she gets into a new relationship she really means it. She will show you all of the love that you will ever need. So don't fight it, let it grow naturally.

If your wife makes more money than you, thank God for the blessing. Because it is truly a blessing. If she makes more money than you, don't get mad, get over it, do cartwheels and back flips because it is a wonderful thing. If you accept it and respect her earning power, she will never throw it into your face. Allow her to have her own money, her own bank account, her own car. If you do, she will worship you and whatever is hers is yours.

Husbands and wives should never tell each other that they don't need each other, because where there is love, there is need. I can love you without totally trusting you. As a man I am giving you 99%, please let me have the 1%, that 1% is my sanity.

When the children arrive, let them gravitate towards their mother. Just throw your contribution into the fray as you go along. Kids will always take from both of you, some woman can raise children on their own, some cannot. But having a man in the mist is necessary, but it may not be mandatory. A woman is complex, you must understand the complexity of a woman when it comes to the children there is a special bond between a mother and her children, Why? because the children were conceived in their mother's womb. She doesn't necessarily know how to let go. It's up to her to allow her children some independence. Please don't let that make you feel bad. So, when the child wakes up at 3:00 AM in the morning, you get up, don't always expect your wife to get up. Those are the small opportunities early on you have where you can make an imprint on your child's life. Most importantly, those are the moments when the child can make some early imprints on you. But if you think it is totally your wife's job in those situations, well, you are missing out on a terrific opportunity to continue a solidification of your marriage. Remember, the mother is the nurturer, but the father will help that child develop a personality, without you, daddy, the child will take longer to develop their personality. The child needs their father to help them to begin to develop who they

FINDING YOUR NITCH, A GUIDE FOR STAY AT HOME FATHERS

are. Because, if a man really takes this fatherhood thing seriously, eventually his grandchildren will call him dad. All of the children in the neighborhood gravitate towards the home where the good fathers reside. All good fathers will become the fathers of many. This is crucial because these are the young men and women whom your children hang out with, these are your children's peers, who they talk to, go to school with and even marry. So you want to have some sort of influence on all of the children in the neighborhood. Just strive to be in a position to set the right example for all children. So be a good father and become the father of many.

As fathers we have to realize that we cannot be dedicated to anything other that our homes. You cannot go to bed at night in a marriage thinking stupid. You must take your job as the head of household seriously and have a plan for the strengthening of your family. That face which is lying next to you wakes you up in the morning. She is your motivation, she knows that she can depend on you for whatever that she might need for the household. If you don't have that mindset, you will lose. Your wife deserves that you go above and beyond for her. You have to believe that she deserves it. That belief will keep you together, if you truly want to give her what she deserves. If you do she will give you whatever you want and need to be successful.

A real Black Man will deal with anything, it is our job to take care of the Black Woman. I showed my wife that I can build a home. So I built my home around my wife. I didn't have to be a millionaire to build my wife a home. I engineered my life around my wife. It wasn't about the sex. I am proud of the fact that I decided to build my home around my wife. Nothing will make you happier, than if you make a decision to build your home around your wife. You will never experience total happiness until you decide to build a home around the person that you love. I couldn't go the other way, I was raised that way. I was taught to make a decision and to live with it. I would rather that my wife depended on me than me depending on her. But, I do depend on her words saying things like "it's going to be alright" or simple things like, "how was your day", that's all I need to hear. You see, financially I attempt to handle everything, I don't even look at my wife's paycheck. That gives her a strong sense of security and control. She knows that no matter what happens I've got her back and she has mine.

Its hard being a Black man in America and it's even harder to be a Married Black Man in America. Some say three strikes and you're out. I always pray for an additional strike. So take it one day at a time, never putting to much pressure on yourself. Just take today as you took yesterday. Just go about your business. Your wife and children depend on it. They see what you do and they emulate it.

Lesson # One: In times of trouble, reach back for that thing that brought you together.

Lesson # Two: Empower your wife and she will empower you.

Junior

Junior and his lovely wife have been together for more than 40 years. I marvel at how he describes their relationship.

How wonderful it was at the beginning when I found the woman that I desired to marry. As I began to plan for our future together, everything I thought about led us to the actual ceremony. It was a little funny when the minister gave anyone the opportunity to say whatever they needed to say during the ceremony, the only thing that I remember saying was "I do". When I walked out of that ceremony, I felt like we were in a cocoon. Actually that's what it was, because at that point, me and my lovely new wife began to grow together. That's was my beginning philosophy, we felt that we were destined to be together. In fact, we made up of our minds to that destiny. Even though we knew that there would be trials and tribulations we decided that we were going to make this thing last forever. I for one never held on to the fact that my father's marriage didn't last. I knew we had to grow and I had my own idea of what I wanted my marriage to be and because of that we have and continue to have a great life together. We have come so far in our relationship, because we knew from the beginning that there were certain things we had to do to make it last.

We made an effort never to let the things that happened to other couples to affect our marriage. You see. many couples were not staying together and we use the news of their breakups to enhance our marriage. We were actually driven to get closer because of what was happening to others. That is an important thing to understand. Don't ever associate other persons problems with yours, because most of the time those problems don't exist in your relationships unless you create them.

One day something really happened that changed my life and my marriage forever. I was about twenty one years old and a newly married man. It was at this age when I lost my mother. My mother was terminally ill and in a nursing home. I remember getting to the nursing home one day and I was told by the staff that mother had past away. I asked could I go into her room and see her and the attendant said yes, but remember "she is dead". I said ok but I just want to see her. When I got into the room and looked at my mother, she opened her yes and said "take care of Tiny". I'll never forget that even though they said mother was dead, she looked up at me reminding me to take care of my wife. How special was that, that the last thing my supposedly dead mother told me was to take care of my wife, and I said "ok mother".

Early on we had plenty of experiences, I worked at the Worlds Fair and my wife was a beautician, we found an apartment and began our life together. My wife was a superstar, a celebrity, everywhere she went she turns heads. She even did some modeling for a while. But through all of the celebrity, all of the glamour, she never lost her humility. She is such a humble, hulsome person.

Sometimes because she was so beautiful, I might even get feelings of unfaithfulness or infidelity. I would really never ever mean it, I was just so grateful that god put such a wonderful person in my life. If there were ever any suspicions it was based on guilt. Because as a man you would never say something is happening unless you believe that it can actually happen. Never accuse your wife of anything that you are not doing, if you do, that is a bad sign.

You should show your wife respect. What do I mean, I mean never, ever desire another woman. There are a lot of women out there and those types of desires will destroy your marriage. If you start to desire other women your marriage will come to an end. I know it is hard, because it seems as if we were trained to desire other women, it is as if it was planted in us. Look at Tiger Woods, Kobe Bryant, and OJ Simpson, why haven't we changed. We should have learned something from other's experiences. If you do learn from others mistakes your marriage will last. Remember these things were set up to destroy relationships, don't fall into those traps. You have to make up your mind that what you have is much, much better than anything out there. We should display better discipline, do not let things like television promote promiscuous activities. All shows on television seem to be promoting uncommitted sexual relationships. But as a strong man you should keep your composure, there even may be setbacks. But a setback is a setup for a comeback.

Remember to respect you wife. Hanging out all night long is a no no. Even if you are with your friends, don't do it. As a married man there are certain things that you cannot do. Staying out all night is one of those things. In life you should always focus on the positive, never ever focus on the negative. If you focus on the positive, positive things will flow into you relationship.

A good wife will never ask you where you have been, most of the time she already knows. Your wife is always two or three steps ahead of you. You never have to make up a story about your actions, because if you do she will never forget and you will have to keep that lie and you are not capable of doing that so don't make up any stories, be truthful.

When we started to have children we didn't skip a beat. We showed little concern for the changes and adjusted our lifestyles because we were in love with each other. You have to be conscious of the changes and make the adjustment as smoothly as possible. It's no big deal; children always arrive in relationships eventually. It won't be easy but, we didn't let anything get in our way. We were on a mission towards fulfillment and happiness. You see, during her first pregnancy, my wife got sick early on, and I tried to be there for her all along the way. It was a new experience for both of us and I was determined to handle it. So when our first child came we just focused on the child, together. We had bigger things to think about. Take your challenges head on. You will be happier for it. We have three children and we continue to have a great marriage and a great life.

As you get older you get much wiser, embrace it, especially as it relates to your children. Realize that you are wiser now and that you know some things that others don't. When the children started going to school, I was the parent who went to the schools. Fathers need to go to their children's schools, **TEACHERS AND OTHER SCHOOL ADMINISTRATORS NEED TO SEE THE FATHERS.**

As my family grew and the children started to get older, I always wanted to know what they were talking about. When I came home from work I would listen at the door for a few minutes before knocking so that I can know what everybody was talking about. I did that for years and was always knowledgeable about the conversations which were going on in my home. This gave me a heads up on what was happening in my home. Another thing, if you are not going to stop your children from listening to Rap Music, you better start listening yourself. Anything that your children are involved in, you better be involved in. Those outside influences could be feeding death to your children and you need to know.

My wife was never noisy. She never nagged me or called me out of my name. I never called her out of her name.

Men, never say something to your wife that you might regret later, words hurt and they never, ever forget. Even though your family approved of your wife and your friends approve of your wife, if you don't show her the proper respect, nobody will.

Finally, from the time your children begin to read, teach them how to spell the word RESPONSIBIL_TY. You left out the "I", point that out to them that "I" is the missing ingredient. You must be responsible fathers, responsible husbands because responsibility is the missing ingredient in all failed relationships. If you teach responsibility, you will build great families, great communities and a great nation. Every institution in this country, churches, schools, the media etc., should be teaching responsibility without the "I"

Lesson # One: Don't pay attention to people less committed than you.

Lesson # Two: Start teaching you children how to spell the word RESPONSIBIL_TY without the "I" as soon as they learn to read.

KANE

The most important thing to understand is that you have to be friends. Being friends will allow you to develop and to learn to compromise. You will agree on some things, you will disagree on some things, but the majority of time you will agree because you like each other. You need to start thinking what is yours is mine what is mine is yours and everything is ours. Your personal things become things that each of us have together. You must get away from the idea that it is two people, it is now us.

When the children started to arrive, things became much different. But you have to have discipline. Sometimes it is a strain because my beliefs and her beliefs are different. You see, I didn't have a father, so I always said that I would do my children differently. The funny thing is, I didn't know what to do. You can look at your father and say, I will be different. Some times you can reflect on what your father did or did not do and work towards being a better father. With the children you can sometimes work towards being friends with them, sometimes being a disciplinarian or not. Sometimes it works sometimes it doesn't. But I have always been tough on my kids. No compromise when it comes to school, chores and respect for people and their elders. I am like that because I want them to be successful. I want them to be the best. In my opinion, most of the time I have been right. You see, today kids have so much to do, so many distractions and they need specific, focused direction.

Sometimes women have babies just to keep men in their lives. That is the wrong way to go. If I have any, I will always teach my daughters differently. But mostly with children you have to learn to listen.

Anytime I need some direction or advice or even advice I need to give out, I look to my wife, she is always there to guide me. She is my conscious on my shoulder. She reminds me not to try to be something that I am not. Keep your eyes on the prize stay focused. If you do everything that you need to do in your marriage, the pieces will fall in place. Stay on yourself first, keep making yourself better and if you do, you will be able to move in the right direction in your marriage. For one, I believe that my wife and I were meant to be. When I first saw her I said to myself, "I'm going to marry that girl". We were meant to be, and 25 years later I am still married to that girl. That's because we were friends long before we fell in love. That is a prerequisite, "you must be friends first". A funny thing always happens to me, when I run into some of my old friends they say, "you still married to that girl?", and I say of course she is the love of my life. Always asking "you still married", I just look at them and smile and say "you can do it too".

Looking around at all of these young girls with children and no husbands, I am reminded that if they would have just worked on themselves, just took the time to get an education, get a job, some security on their own, they might have been able to marry without having children first. Please take the time to take care of yourself first and everything will follow properly. Do you first; education, job, shelter and some money and then you will find the person that you need. Your expectations might be too high, because everybody wants a relationship, but sometimes people decide to move on. That's ok if you have decided to take care of you. You should think about your integrity and not other priorities. If you take care of yours, you will be in a position to pick the proper mate, not the other way around. In my experiences women want to do the right thing. So if you want to do the right thing, your mate will gravitate towards you.

Men you can't hustle forever. You must get your education and do something positive because you can't get anywhere without it. Even though it is not real cool to be a boy and smart these days, you have to work and get rid of that stereotype. Remember, as men we have certain standards. Don't be sifting through all of these girls because some of them are bad choices. It is the choices you make that will determine your future. All of those bad choices will influence you when the right companion comes into your life. So fathers talk to your sons, tell them how to make the right choices. Set the right example by settling for one great lady. Show her love in front of your sons, be the right example and your son's will follow in your footsteps.

Lesson # One – Be friends first

Lesson # Two – Do U

Rome

Marriage is a give and take scenario. I realized that because I had no clue I was going to marry this woman. My initial reaction was totally visual, she looked good and I wanted it. It was such a superficial way in which I met my wife that I am almost embarrassed talking about how shallow I was back then. You see, I quickly discovered that she was much more of substance. What a personality? After I discovered her personality, I realized that if I married her I would be marrying someone that was so much different than any woman I have ever met before. She had qualities that amazed me. She came from a good family, was raised so decent and so well cultured that I was overwhelmed. I was so enthralled with her that I didn't realize that marriage is not a fairy tale. I don't believe that my new wife understood that either. We both had unrealistic expectations of marriage. It took the understanding of my wife to bring me back to reality. At first this marriage was real rough. It got to the point where she would run home to her mother, and I would bring her back. It happened a few times until one day something very special happened. My wife wanted to go to the handball court to be with some friends. I said no you can't go, you have to stay home with the kids, she said she was going and as their father you can stay home with them. So I had the ordacity to lie down in front of the door to prevent her from leaving. All of a sudden I saw stars. My wife had busted me upside my head with a vase. I was dazed and disoriented but when I finally got myself together I apologized to my wife for making her hit me like that. You see, I realized that she is a grown woman and I can't dictate to her. She has the right to do as she pleases. At that point I started to work on my marriage. I made a decision to make it work. Even after all of that, I wouldn't change a thing; I don't regret anything that happened. It made me appreciate this great woman. At this point I realized that we were meant to be together.

If you really want to appreciate your wife, make sure you go into the delivery room when your children are being born. Just to realize that this woman, my wife is willing to go through the agony of child birth for me, for the birth of my children, I just couldn't believe the level of love she had for me. After the children were born, my wife took off weeks from work to take care of our kids. My wife got up late at night when the children needed something. My wife this, my wife that, I took this woman for granted and I wish I could have spent more time during my children's nurturing period. She gave so much of herself. Sometimes I feel envious of a mother's love. So now I pay strict attention to her. Knowing that I could never bring back that time, but making the time we have together as pleasant as possible. In this world fathers have the opportunity to live differently than mothers and some fathers take advantage of that situation. So with my kids I try to be there physically and also I am attempting to add my emotional part to our relationship. I am really putting in more emotion than I have in the past.

My examples in life were few. My earliest memories of my father were him beating my mother. Until a few years ago I hadn't seen my father since I was 8 years old and now I am nearly 50. One day I got a call saying that my father was very sick. Since I never held anything against him, I went to see him. When I got there I saw that he was all alone, he didn't have anyone or anything to speak of. So I planned to bring him to New York to make sure that he had everything that he might need. I wanted to reconcile with him so I straightened out all of his affairs, brought him into my home and nursed him back to health. He got better and began to demand things. Mainly, he wanted to visit his sister in the Bronx. So I let him visit her. Differently from my home he was allowed to engage in some unsavory behavior in the Bronx. They allowed him to drink and smoke, two things that were a major impediment to his health. I did not allow him to do those things in my house, but they allowed him to do them in the Bronx. So when he came back home with us he kept wanting to go back to the Bronx where he could do anything that he wanted. I was very interested in keeping my father healthy but this struggle began to affect my marriage. You see, I wanted to create a legacy for my father, because when I was young every time I depended on him for something he would always disappoint me. I made up my mind to never disappoint my kids. I will never promise my kids anything that I couldn't do. So I sent my father back to Florida, where I hear that he is very sick again. My father taught me a very good lesson. He taught me how not to be a father. I thank him for that very important lesson.

When I was growing up I always wanted to be dressed, to be fly. I always wanted to wear the best clothes and look good for the ladies. When I had my first child, I never went to the store again. I wanted to set the best example for my children. Even though they might have thought that I was mean, I was just a disciplinarian. I know people who thought that their parents were mean and today wish they had the opportunity to tell their parents how much they appreciated the discipline. So if God has given you that opportunity, please take the time to tell them how grateful you are, because nobody lives forever.

I realize that I gave my kids all of the tools that they needed to succeed, but it is up to them to use those tools. I can't use hindsight to redesign my life, but I know that as long as I have my wife, my back is covered. Man, she is wonderful and I thank God everyday for allowing her to come into my life.

When I look back and point out the time in my life that made me realize what a good woman I had. I actually took a moment to examine her. I mean really, objectively examine my wife. What I found is that she is head and shoulders above any woman that I have ever had a relationship with. My wife is driven and stands out upon comparisons with any woman. My wife has such good qualities that when I thought I was going to lose her, I got physically sick. She has all of the qualities that I needed in a woman to help me strive and get ahead in life. To tell someone where I came from, with all of the lazy, uninspired women I have had in my life. How some women don't even think about the future, I have struck gold. This wife of mine is at the top of quality of women. Finally, this is the truth and I will always tell people about her. I have a powerful consistent message, appreciate your good woman; you may never get another chance if you let her go.

Lesson # One: Your wife is grown so you cannot dictate to her.

Lesson # Two: Go into the delivery room and watch your children being born, you will appreciate her dedication to you.

Section III

The Foundation

Certainty

One of the most astonishing developments in relationships over the past 30 years is that they don't last. Even more astonishing is the reasons people give for the dissolution of their relationships. Many people believe that monetary difficulties lead to the breakup of relationships. They believe that any difficulties that disrupt the procurement of resources for the family unit lead to breakups. I too believe that monetary issues are important because they inevitably affect standard of living. But I have seen people who are literally broke and homeless displaying high levels of devotion and affection towards one another. In fact, many of them site their lack of resources as the reason they remain together, I guess it is a "needs thing". So maybe monetary considerations can be sited as reason number one in any number of breakups, but from my observations some of the best couples, ones that have been together for years struggle everyday just to eat and pay their bills, but they still manage to keep the relationships strong. They still mange to display a high level of companionship.

Since we are on a subject that relates directly to love, let's discuss it. Many of you are going to think that I am crazy but LOVE IS OVERATED. That's right I said it, love is overrated. But by the same token lust is underrated. Why, because I believe that love covers a multitude of sins. Love in essence does not allow us to view our long term relationships with honesty, clarity and with an open mind. You see, if I happen to be head over heels in love with someone, in other words committing my entire heart, soul and mind to them. I am less likely to pay attention to that person's faults. As the saying goes "love is blind", I suffice to say love is "TOTALLY BLIND". Because in long term relationships of imperfect human beings, faults always rise to the surface. I'm not saying that you shouldn't love the person that you wish to marry, all I am saying is that you should be very aware of the limitations that love places on the objective, practical mind.

On the other hand lust is vastly underrated. Most people foolishly say that they would rather have someone love them for 20 years than to have them lust after them for 20 years. On the other hand it is important to be able to distinguish the differences at first. Because I believe that a person who expresses love for you early on in a relationship, usually lusts after you excessively. I submit to you that lust is probably the most vital part in the sustaining of a long term relationship. I have a little lesson on how to use it to sustain your relationship. When you meet a person who displays all of the physical attributes that you desire, automatically your human patent for lust kicks in. You can't get enough of that person. I use to tell my future wife "baby, I just can't get close enough". So you lust after this person, convincing both of you that you are in love, you get married and you experience what a good friend of mind called "the last passionate kiss". You still love this person and you both continue trudging along handing towards eventual separation or not.

This is the solution to the love/lust thing. First of all you don't have to be head over heels in love with someone to marry them. Because most of it is blind lust. You should marry them but with a keen eye on all of her attributes, i.e. her education, the way she treats other people, her ideas about life and most importantly, her physical, emotional and psychological flaws. If you do this you will have made a "conscious" decision to accept her with her flaws and she has to make the same types of determinations as it relates to you. Because brother married is real, this is no game and it is a two way street. Brother, listen very closely to what am about to say now because this is the most important lesson you will ever learn on how to use this love/lust thing to make your married last forever. Firstly, when you get married and you really, really want this thing to last, you have to make a conscious effort to lust after your wife for "5 consecutive years". I mean it has to be in your plans, because it won't happen automatically. Even on days when you don't feel like it, lust after her, even if you have to keep a "daily lust diary", do it. In that diary you should set of a lust schedule where you know that these things are going to happen and that they are targeted. I don't mean having sex, because that is the easy part and you will find that it could get quite boring to her if it is not done in a lustful fashion. Brothers, women get bored of sex very quickly. Remember, not for one year, or two years or even four years, it must be five consecutive years. Believe me if you show your wife your lustful tendencies every day for five consecutive years and you are serious about keeping your marriage together, you do this and after five years you will finally attained the type of love that you need to stay together forever. You see, the lusting exercise is not for your wife it is for you. What this does is fortify your marriage as a strong base of constant interaction between husband and wife. After that, nothing will be able to separate you from your wife and children. Brothers, don't take this lightly, this is one of the main reasons why men decide to leave their children. Some relationships even survive this period of disconnect, leading to many years of unhappy relationships.

Many people say that we couldn't stay together because there is no trust. Fellows, again trust is overrated. It really is. Think about the fact that you would put all of the pressure of trust in to the hands of another imperfect being. Into the hands of another human being. YOU TRUST IN GOD and that's it. Too many relationships break up because of trust issues, when trust is the last thing that you should place in to hands of another. If I can get you to understand one thing in this and that is DON'T TRUST ANYBODY. I'm not telling you to go around with one eye on everybody that is around you or maybe I am, but one thing I do know and that is, trust is too deep an emotion to base your emotional stability on. It will drive you crazy putting your trust in another human being. Someone, who might very well be in love with you, but they are ill-equipped to shoulder such a burden. My life changed forever when I decided not to base my emotional decisions on the trusting of my wife. It not only made me happier, it stabilized my marriage and helped us grow immeasurably. We got closer and became much better people. The joke is that she didn't even realize it had happened. After nearly 30 years of marriage my wife will find out about my decision concerning trust through the reading of this book. So if you think your relationship will last if you base it around trusting another person, wake up and smell the coffee. If you really thought about it, how can you lay such and awesome responsibility onto another person, as if they are responsible for your personal happiness. In this relationship thing you are responsible for your own happiness, she is responsible for hers and when you come together, the happiness is doubled, but not if either of you are carrying the burden of trust. If you do, you are surly headed to crash into the rocks of unhappiness and possibly divorce.

When I realized that monetary considerations were not important in my relationship, that love was overrated and lust was underrated, when I totally stripped myself of the burden of trust. I realized that the only thing that my relationship needed was certainty. I finally realized that most relationships breakup because of the lack of certainty. Let me explain, if you were married to a person whom you weren't sure how they would react under certain circumstances, you would be terribly unsure on how to proceed with them. I'll give you an example, you knew that every Tuesday morning there was something that your significant other was supposed to do and every Tuesday you were unsure whether that task would be accomplished and you were unsure whether that person would even give you a heads up when they became aware that they could not perform. Or supposed every time your wife left the house she gave you a kiss and this had been happening for years and then all of a sudden she stopped, your certainty would be severely damaged. If it was your job to pick up the children everyday, but your spouse wasn't sure whether you would do it consistently, that brings uncertainty into your relationship. You say that's this is just another way of talking about trust. But no it isn't, there is a very distinct difference. Trust puts the burden on the other person to behave talk and conduct themselves in a particular manner. Certainty puts the burden on you. In relationships, the more you take the emotional burdens off of our partners and place them upon ourselves, the stronger your relationships become, you begin to incorporate personal responsibility into it. In a nut shell, if your relationship continues to be chipped away by uncertainty, no amount of love, lust, money or any other material things will keep you together. Finally and most importantly, children depend on the certainty of their parents to feel secure. Most relationships which contain large amounts of uncertainty usually produce unruly, undisciplined children. Because the children begin to take on the mantle of certainty far beyond their means and capacity. So men focus like a laser beam on certainty and your marriage will last forever.

Lesson # One: Money, Love and Trust is Overrated, Lust is Underrated

Lesson # Two: Certainty in a relationship, puts the burdens in the right place, squarely on your shoulders

THE NITCH

Let us talk about a hypothetical father. A father who loves his wife and cherishes his children, but he like many fathers have come to the realization of worthlessness. You see, mothers have come to represent the epitome of parenting. Both children and fathers alike gravitate towards their warm motherly love. It is a wonderful thing in which nature has planted us. Mothers are the nuturers and fathers are the providers, at least it seems the way nature planned it.

Let me explain, when people fall in love and they decide to get married in most cases they are operating out of the uncontrolled lust that they have for each other. Everything is bliss and happiness. Two people in love, running, frolicking, sharing and playing with each other, actually becoming soul mates. Suddenly and decision is made to build a family, to have children. When the children begin to arrive, fathers finally get the chance to experience unconditional love. Man, this is the apex of happiness, the joyful weight of responsibility and pride begins to feel your entire being. You look forward to teaching and training your children, in fact you plan their entire development in your mind everyday. You go to bed every night thinking how your children will grow up to conquer the world and how you will be the kingmaker.

As time goes by you notice how the children begin to gravitate towards the mother. You don't pay much attention to it because you understand that mothers are the nurturers and you believe that this is natural.

Some couples start trying to get back to the way it was before they had children. Listen to me, YOU WILL NEVER GO BACK TO THOSE DAYS SO DON'T TRY. That is not the problem. You still love each other; you just have other people in the mix to share your love with. Your wife doesn't realize it but other things are going through your mind.

Soon you begin to realize that the only part that you play in this house is as the breadwinner. You go to work everyday, you come home, make sure that all of the bills are paid, offer security to your wife and children, but your role in the nurturing process has diminished In fact you begin to feel that you can serve this

37

role from across the street, across town or even across country. You start to believe that you don't have to be here to fulfill you capacity in this household.

At this point, stop, think and reevaluate your role. This is a turning point in your family life and your must conquer it. You have to consciously find your Nitch. Even if you have to fight for it (I don't mean physically). What I do mean is this. There are so many things within that household other then the typical breadwinner duties that you can step in, do them and do them so well that if you don't do it, it won't get done... I must repeat that last sentence, *your nitch must be something that if you don't do it, it won't get done.* One father told me that it was his responsibility to read to his children at a certain time every night and he made sure that they expected it. One father said that he took total control of his children's athletic habits and coached them in any sport he could think of, another said that it was him who made sure that he never, ever missed an open school night for 22 years and his children used to wait for him at school each time. What's so amazing about this theory fathers is that your wives begin to fall right into place and they begin to depend on you to accomplish these feats. So much so that they begin to establish their own nitches around yours, so there is never any conflict. You begin what I call Certainty discussed earlier in this book.

Have fun with establishing your nitch, play around with it, watch how you family adjusts to it. It will make you happy and most importantly, your family unit will be stronger and last longer.

Lesson One: This is an extremely important turning point.

Lesson Two: FIND YOUR NITCH

In Conclusion

As a man who has had the privilege of sharing my love with one very special person. I am absolutely sure that as Kane says "you can do it too". There is no secret formula, just a series of reasoned, impassioned decisions with the intent of being successful. If you do this I guarantee you, you will have a strong, loving family life.

I have been thinking about this book over a number of years. Not because of my concern for the stabilization of the family unit, but mostly because our children effect the lives of many generations to come. We as fathers must realize that not only are we responsible for our children but we are responsible for all children. That our conduct as fathers makes an imprint of young peoples lives everywhere, and as Junior says, we have to want to live the "I" of responsibil_ty.

Whether it comes down to your wife's decisions or the acknowledgement that the absence of "certainty" in your relationship has caused problems or that the sexual preference of your children or any one of your family members affects the way you love them. You will never be able to compartmentalize your life if it is not a conscious decision. This is not brain surgery, it's simple but it is not easy. It takes sacrifice, understanding and the willingness to come to grips with the fact that you are an imperfect being, making imperfect decisions.

Find your **Nitch**, not just in love but in life. Find that one conveyor that will lead you to a happier, more productive existence. It might be multiple things, all leading you to your goal of self fulfillment and success. Finding your **Nitch** will help you find that thing that will make you happy, help you to love yourself and gain a feeling of accomplishment. You will make mistakes in life, but remember, FORGIVE YOURSELF OVER, AND OVER, AND OVER AND OVER AGAIN…... Finding you **Nitch** will help you understand that you should be designing your life and not just making a living. Your **Nitch** will help you, design it, shape it, model it and create the type of discipline which is solely needed in relationships. I am convinced that if not for the finding of my **Nitch,** which allowed me to find a permanent spot in my family's affairs, not only would I not be married, but quite possibly, I would be dead.